Anonymous

The Battle Fields of the Maumee Valley

Anonymous

The Battle Fields of the Maumee Valley

ISBN/EAN: 9783744743822

Printed in Europe, USA, Canada, Australia, Japan

Cover: Foto ©ninafisch / pixelio.de

More available books at **www.hansebooks.com**

OF THE

MAUMEE VALLEY

A COLLECTION OF HISTORICAL ADDRESSES
DELIVERED BEFORE

THE SONS OF THE AMERICAN REVOLUTION,

DISTRICT OF COLUMBIA SOCIETY,

MARCH 18, 1896.

WASHINGTON CITY
1896

INTRODUCTION.

By Dr. G. Brown Goode,

President of the District of Columbia Society,
Sons of the American Revolution.

THE Society of the Sons of the American Revolution was organized to take part in measures tending to foster the development of American patriotism, among which a not unimportant one is the preservation of historic sites and marking them by monuments.

The War of the Revolution did not cease with the treaty of Paris, but continued until the conquest of the West had been accomplished and the rights of our people secured by the success of our second conflict with Great Britain. It is, therefore, very appropriate that we should listen to-night to a series of papers on the acquisition of the Northwest and the struggle with the Indians and Great Britain, up to and including the War of 1812.

This region was traversed during the War of the Revolution by that intrepid soldier George Rogers Clark. He, with his band of Kentuckians, met the Indians at Harrodsburg in 1776, defeated them in 1777, and ultimately in 1779 compelled the British commander at Vincennes to capitulate. Thus was ended the English occupancy, and thus were made possible the negotiations for the possession of the vast regions beyond the Alleghenies subsequently conceded by Great Britain.

The papers to be read this evening relate to these battles in the Northwest. Bills are now before Congress providing for the permanent preservation, as the property of the Nation, of the ground upon which these battles were fought. This is a matter of national importance, not only on account of historical association, but because here are buried over two thousand soldiers from every State then in the Union. The securing of these sites will be equivalent to the erection of permanent monuments to the memory of men and events of the utmost significance in the history of the struggle of " the winning of the West."

It is little less than a national disgrace that there should have been no monuments erected to commemorate these battles, so important to the history of the United States.

The more formal papers of the evening will be preceded by a brief address on Indian methods of warfare intended to make the narratives which follow more intelligible.

Methods of Indian Warfare.

By Professor Otis T. Mason,

Smithsonian Institution.

B Y WAY of introduction to the addresses of the distinguished speakers who are to follow me, I have been invited to make some remarks upon the Indian tribes engaged in the wars about Maumee River, and their methods of fighting.

There were three great stocks of Indians centering in this portion of the northwest territory; the Algonquian stock covered the largest area, embracing eastern and southern Canada, the New England States, Maryland, Virginia, and the territory drained by the Ohio River and the eastern tributaries of the Mississippi. These Indians depended partly upon agriculture and partly upon hunting and fishing for their subsistence.

The Iroquoian stock was to be found on both sides of the Upper Saint Lawrence River and all about Lake Ontario, Lake Erie, and the southern shores of Lake Huron. Some of their weaker tribes had pushed their way to the head waters of the Chesapeake Bay. A large branch of the Iroquoian stock was to be found also in the mountain region where the States of Virginia, Tennessee, Carolina, and Georgia meet.

On the west side of the Algonquian were the Siouan tribes, who resided mostly west of the Mississippi River and reached as far as the western shore of Lake Michigan.

Before describing the methods of warfare practiced by all of the Indians of these three stocks, it is well to remember that in war there are only three methods of killing a man, namely, by piercing weapons, by cutting weapons, by bruising weapons. These were represented in pre-Columbian times by the war spear, the stone knife or dagger, and clubs of various kinds. As soon as these Indians entered into trade relationship with the whites, whether English, Dutch, French or Spanish, in exchange for their furs they received muskets and bullets to replace their arrows, swords, scalping knives as substitutes for their stone knives, and cannon balls for clubs. In the use of these the savages soon became proficient, and it is no disparagement to the brave soldiers who conducted for many years the wars in the northwest, to say that the various tribes engaged fought desperately with these new weapons for their homes. As to their tactics they had none, if we judge them from the point of view of European warfare. In point of fact, they lived in that primitive state of society in which the fighting against men and wild beasts have not been differentiated. It was customary for them to select some spot where the deer were wont to frequent and alongside of the valley leading to this place they placed rude fences made of strong poles. Through this drive they effectually enticed and forced their victims until the latter were in an

mbuscade where they were quickly and energeti-
ally dispatched.

The Indian, therefore, used for his tactics
nethods similar to those employed in hunting
he deer, the bear, and the wolf. His strategy
onsisted of the same ingenious device, by means
f which he inveigled the white man into an am-
uscade just as successfully as he allured animals
nto traps. We are not surprised, therefore, in
eading the history of the campaigns in the
Northwest to learn that over and over again many
f the best troops were destroyed by being lead
nto ambushes. It was the Indian's method of
ntrapping a wild beast applied to warfare with.
hose who were better equipped with firearms.
They did not acquire the tactics and strategy of
he white man, but employed new weapons with
ld methods.

It is not within my province to discuss methods
f Indian strategy, although it could be easily
lemonstrated that the white man, knowing the
actics of the civilized warfare, repeatedly adopted
he methods of the savage. The aboriginal tribes
lad the misfortune to ally themselves with the
French against the English and subsequently with
he English against the Americans, and as a result
vere twice deprived of their land by an inter-
national code which was unknown to them.

At the close of the last century the Indians in
he Northwest, instigated by foreign foes, fought
vith desperation against the Americans the last
great fight for the possession of the aboriginal
homes.

Settlement of the Northwest Territory,

WITH THE STRUGGLES AGAINST THE INDIANS AND BRITISH
IN THE MAUMEE VALLEY, 1788–1813.

By MR. WILLIAM VAN ZANDT COX,

NATIONAL MUSEUM.

THE West has been so busy in making History that it has been compelled to leave it to Eastern writers to chronicle. Have they done their part as satisfactorily as the makers? I am free to confess that no series of events in the entire history of this Country has been more completely lost sight of than those between 1788–1813, by means of which the results of the War of the Revolution were confirmed to this Country.

It is surprising to find in the "Narrative and Critical History of America," edited by so able a writer as Justin Winsor, that no prominence is given to those campaigns that gave to America the empire of the Northwest. Indeed so little importance is attached to them that in the article on "Wars of the United States between 1789–1851" only nine and one-half lines are given to the Harmer, St. Clair, and Wayne Campaigns (Vol. VII, p. 357). Something, however, is said in the appendix by the editor. In contrast, the War with Tripoli fills eighteen pages.

The hope of American history is in the Patriotic Societies, the members of which are doing so

A. St. Clair

much to encourage historical research and preserve the memories of the men who achieved the independence of the American people.

I have always considered myself fortunate in having been born in the State of Ohio. When I reflect that I was born on the banks of the Muskingum, made memorable in 1788 by the landing of the boat containing Rufus Putnam's band of pioneers, the "Mayflower of the great Northwest," I know that I am a subject for congratulation.

Of whom did this earnest band of home-seekers and home builders consist?

They were soldiers of the Revolution, the American Revolution, together with their wives and their children, destined by an all wise Providence to be the founders of new American States.

"Fresh from the Revolution's fire
They came, to hew the empire's way
   Through trackless wastes and to inspire
The sunlight of young Freedom's day."

Five states in the Northwest Territory were founded. The names of these are also American: Ohio, Indiana, Illinois, Michigan and Wisconsin, a galaxy of peerless states in the history of our Nation, that stand resplendant as the stars on the blue field of our Country's flag.

These brave men and women, still filled with the courage of '76, were, as events show, equal to the task before them. Like their pilgrim fathers, they felled the trees of the forests and built their homes; with their trusty rifles by their sides, they cleared the ground and planted their corn. They endured hardships that only men and women would be willing to suffer for the sake of conscience, homes and liberty.

Foes lurked on every side, for in these forests dwelt the Shawnees, the Chippewas, the Delawares, the Ottawas, the Wyandots, the Pottawatomis and the warlike Miamis, who, instigated by the British, were quick to form alliance against the new settlers. For two years the Frontiersmen suffered from scalping knife and tomahawk, and then a small body of regulars enlisted in Pennsylvania and New Jersey, were placed under the command of General Harmer, with orders to march against the Indian towns and inflict such punishment as would prevent future depredations.

Reinforced by over a thousand of militia from Ohio, Pennsylvania, and Kentucky, General Harmer started from Fort Washington (now Cincinnati) on September 30, 1790, to execute the plans of President Washington.

Harmer, on October 19, met the Indians under Little Turtle at the junction of the St. Mary and St. Joseph rivers, in the present state of Indiana, and was disastrously defeated, failing in his mission and losing many of his brave officers and men.

President Washington was greatly distressed and disappointed at Harmer's misfortune and designated General Arthur St. Clair, the first Governor of the Northwest Territory, who was inaugurated at Marietta July 15, 1788, to take command and surpress the Indian invasions.

On September 17, 1791, with an army numbering twenty-three hundred men, he marched from Fort Washington and erected Fort Hamilton on the Miami, the first of a line of forts that was to extend to Lake Erie. On October 12 the construction of Fort Jefferson was begun. On November 3 the army reached the Wabash. On November 4 Little Turtle, with his warriors, surprised St. Clair and defeated a second army within a year.

When Washington read the message from St. Clair announcing his reverses, it is said that he threw it down and paced the floor in anger, using language that is not considered appropriate for even state occasion.

The Ohio settlements were in terror. The entire Country was aroused at the thought of the veterans of '76 and their families being massacred by the red men and at the instigation of the old enemy, the British.

By popular consent General Anthony Wayne of Pennsylvania, the daring hero of the Revolution, was selected by Washington to protect the frontier. He consented to serve on the condition that he was not to begin his campaign until his ranks were full and his men thoroughly disciplined.

In June, 1792, General Wayne proceeded to Pittsburg and began organizing and vigorously drilling his "Legion."

From Pittsburg he floated his army down the Ohio and established a camp called Hobson's Choice, near Cincinnati. On October 7, 1793, he started on his march to Lake Erie, and soon after he established winter quarters at Fort Greenville, in Darke County.

On Christmas, the place made memorable by St. Clair's defeat was re-occupied... "Here" said he, "where the blood of our brothers has enriched

The battle of Fallen Timber, for such is its name, was fought under the walls of Fort Miami. Alarmed at the defeat of his allies, Major Campbell, commanding the British Post, was anxious to know in what light he was to view Wayne's near approach to his garrison. Wayne wrote him as follows:—"I think I may, without breach of decorum, observe to you, that, were you entitled to an answer, the most full and satisfactory one was announced to you from the muzzles of my small arms, yesterday morning, in the action against the horde of savages in the vicinity of your post, which terminated gloriously to the American arms; but, had it continued until the Indians, etc., were driven under the influence of the post and guns you mention, they would not have much impeded the progress of the victorious army under my command as no such post was established at the commencement of the present war between the Indians and the United States."

Major Campbell replied, saying among other things, "I have forborne, for these two days past, to resent those insults you have offered to the British flag flying at this fort, by approaching within pistol shot of my works, not only singly, but in numbers, with arms in their hands. Neither is it my wish to wage war with individuals; but, should you, after this, continue to approach my post in the threatening manner you are at this moment doing, my indispensable duty to my king and country, and the honor of my profession, will oblige me to have recourse to those measures which thousands of either nation may hereafter have cause to regret."

Thereupon General Wayne called his attention to his occupying a post within the limits of the United States, adding : " This, sir, appears to be an act of the highest aggression, and destructive to the peace and interest of the Union. Hence, it becomes my duty to desire, and I do hereby desire and demand, in the name of the President of the United States, that you immediately desist from any further act of hostility or aggression, by forbearing to fortify, and by withdrawing the troops, artillery, and stores, under your order and direction, forthwith, and removing to the nearest post occupied by His Britannic Majesty's troops at the peace of 1783, and which you will be permitted to do unmolested by the troops under my command."

It was the policy of Great Britain, you will observe, over a hundred years ago, to erect forts and take position and possession on lines other than those prescribed in treaties.

Fort Miami, however, was not attacked by Wayne, his foresight suggesting the desirability of erecting a block house nearer the mouth of the Maumee. This was built and so expeditiously, that he called it Fort Industry, and it is within the limits of Toledo, in the very heart of the city.

On August 27, 1794, the army took up its return march, destroying every village and corn field as far as Defiance.

The Miami villages were reached in turn, and at the very spot where Harmer had been defeated four years previously, a fort was erected, This place now bears the name of Fort Wayne, Indiana.

Having accomplished the objects of his campaign Wayne started with the main body of his army for Fort Greenville.   Here, in negotiating the famous Greenville treaty with thirteen tribes of Indians, he proved himself to be as great a diplomat and statesman as he had shown himself to be a soldier.

On the staff of General Wayne during this campaign was Lieutenant William Henry Harrison, who was destined to achieve eminence and to complete the victories begun by his General.

On September 17, 1812, General Harrison having the year before defeated at Tippecanoe, "The Prophet," brother of Tecumseh, was placed in command of the army of the West and Northwest.

In February, 1813, he arrived on the Maumee and built Fort Meigs.

Early in May this fort was attacked by a force of thirty-two hundred British and Indians under Proctor and Tecumseh.   It was on the west side of the Maumee that Colonel Dudley, while attempting to capture a battery, was ambuscaded and lost his life together with 685 of his 810 impetuous Kentuckians.   Few men taken escaped alive.   It is said that when Tecumseh saw the American prisoners being murdered, he asked Proctor why he had not put a stop to the inhuman massacre, Proctor replied, "your Indians cannot be commanded."   "Begone" said Tecumseh, in thundering tones, "you are unfit to command, go and put on petticoats."

The attack on Fort Meigs continued several days but was finally successfully repelled, the enemy withdrawing to Fort Malden, in Canada, the strategic center of British operations in the Northwest.

In July, largely reinforced, and during General Harrison's absence to Lower Sandusky, the British and Indians again attacked Fort Meigs and for a second time in two months were compelled to raise the siege.

On July 4, General Harrison, remembering the historic date, patriotically ordered a National salute fired in honor of the "return of the day which gave liberty and independence to the United States of America." He ordered men under sentence and in confinement released, Court Martials dissolved, and all troops reported fit for duty were to receive an extra gill of whiskey. It may be inferred that they received it, for the order concludes "this will be fatigue day."

In August, Port Stephenson (now Fremont) was attacked by the British and Indians. Major Croghan, a youth who had just passed his twenty-first year, was in command of the Fort, and wrote to General Harrison, "we have determined to maintain this place, and by heavens we can"— and he did, and was promptly promoted.

Commodore Oliver Hazard Perry, of Rhode Island, had at this time about finished the construction of a flotilla at Erie. His fleet, consisting of the Lawrence and Niagara, carrying twenty guns each, and seven small vessels carrying fourteen guns, had been built, manned, and equipped in the wilderness, men and munitions having been brought from points four hundred miles distant.

He, in the presence of the enemy, succeeded in getting his vessel over the bar into Lake Erie. On this point Knapp says :

"The same course which insured the safety of

O. H. Perry

the ships while building seemed to prevent their being of any service. The two largest drew several feet more water than there was on the bar. The inventive genius of Commodore Perry, however, soon surmounted the difficulty. He placed large scows on each side of the largest ship, filled them so as to sink to the water's edge then attached them to the ship by strong pieces of timber and pumped out the water. The scows then buoyed up the ship so as to pass the bar in safety."

Unfurling sail, Perry proceeded to Put-in-Bay. On September 10, 1813, he hoisted the American jack on the Lawrence. When the crews saw it and read on it the dying words of Captain James Lawrence of the illfated Chesapeake, "Don't give up the ship," they sent up cheer after cheer.

Every ship now prepared for action and at once bore down upon the enemy's fleet.

A terrific fire was opened on the Lawrence, which was not replied to until her short range guns could be brought into effective service.

Keeping on her course her sides were pierced in all directions, men were killed and wounded in every part of the ship. Realizing the danger of his position, Commodore Perry ordered all sail made and renewed his efforts to close in upon the enemy's vessels.

When every brace and bow line on the Lawrence had been shot away and she became unmanageable, the Commodore decided to shift his flag to the Niagara.

A boat was ordered in which with a gallant crew he started on his perilous trip. He reached the Niagara through musketry and broad-sides, and amid cheers, again had the inspiring American jack hoisted.

Orders were issued to the entire fleet for close action. The enemy's ships were hemmed in and raked with grape and cannister until every one had struck its colors. Never was victory more complete.

Perry then wrote his famous despatch, "We have met the enemy and they are ours." The receipt of which General Harrison celebrated by ordering a movement upon Malden, using the captured vessels for transports.

The enemy retreated, but was overtaken on October 5th, a battle was fought and another victory for the Americans gained. Proctor had been put to flight, Tecumseh had been slain, and the supremacy of the Northwest forever established.

The lives of twenty-five hundred American heroes were sacrificed in these engagements against the combined efforts of the Indians and the British, and to-night they sleep in unmarked graves on the shores of Put-in-Bay and on the banks of the Maumee.

Efforts made by the Maumee Valley Monumental Association towards preserving Historic Sites in Northwestern Ohio.

BY HON. JAMES H. SOUTHARD,

MEMBER OF CONGRESS FROM OHIO.

THE condition of the sites of the battle grounds of the Maumee Valley, including the burial places on Put-in-Bay Island, of those who lost their lives in the battle of Lake Erie, is a matter in which the people of our section of the country are, and for sometime past have been, taking a lively interest. It is much to be regretted that these places, important as they are in a historic sense, should have been allowed to pass out of the possession of the general government and into private hands, and to remain without any markings other than the rude designations which have been inspired by the patriotism of those who now own them. It seems almost unaccountable that this should have been permitted. Certainly it cannot be that a people whose pride and patriotism are acknowledged have so soon forgotten the heroic achievements of their countrymen, when those achievements were so important and so far-reaching in their results. General Anthony Wayne's greatest battle and victory over the Indians at Fallen Timber practically reclaimed and saved to the United States what was then known as the great Northwest.

The battle of Lake Erie was the most important naval achievement of the war of 1812. Marble and canvas have been made to do service in commemorating this event. All Americans are proud of the skill, endurance, and bravery of Commodore Perry and his men. The genius of the artist has preserved the memory of that great commander, but the graves of the men who died in that terrible conflict are entirely unmarked and uncared for except in the rudest and most temporary way. It is stated that at one time the share of the plowman was allowed to turn up the bones of these heroes as though they had been the bones of beasts, instead of those of patriots who died in the cause of liberty and justice. Not a little of the fame of General Harrison was won in successfully resisting the two attempts of the allied English and Indians to reduce the stronghold of Fort Meigs in the war of 1812.

Fort Meigs is on the southeast bank of the Maumee River, about twelve miles from its mouth, and near the village of Perrysburg. Fallen Timber is on the opposite bank, and about one and a half miles further up the river, and Fort Miami is also on the opposite side about the same distance down the river. Inside, and immediately without the walls of Fort Meigs, are the graves of those who were killed during the two sieges of this fort, and also many hundred brave Kentuckians of Colonel Dudley's command who were massacred by the English forces under Proctor, and the Indians under Tecumseh, during the early part of the year 1813. Nature has provided these patriots with a beautiful resting place, but not a stone or other protection has been provided, and the exact burial spots are known only by the memory of one or two persons who have been spared beyond the years ordinarily allotted to man. The outlines of Fort Meigs are well preserved, as are also those of Fort Miami.

Among the other places of historic interest in the Maumee Valley, is Fort Wayne, in the State of Indiana, where General Harmer suffered defeat with terrible loss in 1790. Fort Defiance, at the junction of the Maumee and Auglaize Rivers, was built by Anthony Wayne in 1794, and Fort Industry was built in the same year.

In 1885 an organization was formed and incorporated known as the Maumee Valley Monumental Association, the object of which is to procure the acquirement by the government of these several sites, and the marking of the same by appropriate monuments, and to otherwise disseminate and perpetuate a knowledge of the important historical facts and events of the Maumee Valley. Chief Justice Morrison R. Waite was the first president of the association, and to the time of his death was an active promoter of the work for which it was formed.

In 1888 the Secretary of War was authorized and directed by act of Congress to cause an "examination and inspection to be made of the historic grounds, locations, and military works of the Maumee Valley." In pursuance of which, a survey and map of each of said sites was made and embodied in a report to Congress in December of that year. The efforts of the Maumee Valley Monumental Association have resulted in arousing a sentiment in favor of purchasing and preserving these historic places. At the centennial celebration of the victory of Anthony Wayne at Fallen Timber August 20th, 1894, it is said that more than ten thousand people were present. The association holds a meeting annually on one of these historic spots, and the meetings are always large and enthusiastic.

Less than one hundred years ago northwestern Ohio was a dense forest and the Maumee Valley was very sparsely settled, but now the territory comprised within a radius of one hundred and twenty-five miles contains at least three or four million people. Fort Meigs and Fort Miami, and Fallen Timber are located near thriving villages, and are easily accessible by rail and by water. Put-in-Bay Island has become a summer resort, and is visited annually by thousands coming from all parts of the country.

Many patriotic and enterprising citizens of the States of Ohio, Indiana, and elsewhere, have taken part in the effort to secure the purchase and preservation of these sites, prominent among whom may be mentioned the Hon. D. W. H. Howard, whose voice and pen have been earnestly employed for many years in the endeavor to arouse public interest in the preservation of their historic grounds, and the Hon. Samuel F. Hunt, of Cincinnati, whose addresses at the centennial gatherings at Fort Washington, Fort Recovery, Fort Defiance and Fallen Timber are chapters in the history of this period. The knowledge that the Sons of the American Revolution are taking an active part in the good work gives assurance that something will be accomplished in the near future.

The Present Condition of the Historic Sites in the Maumee Valley and on the Island of Put-in-Bay.

By Colonel W. H. Chase,

Of the Ohio Society of the Sons of the American Revolution.

THE present condition of the historic sites in the Maumee Valley and on the Island of Put-in-Bay is the subject I bring before you to-night. If you were to take a boat ride from Lake Erie down through Maumee Bay, twelve miles from the Lake you would first land almost opposite Fort Industry, where now stands the thriving city of Toledo with 125,000 inhabitants. Seven miles south of Fort Industry on the west bank of the Maumee you would come to what was known as Fort Miami. Follow the river three miles farther south, you will find on the west bank of the river the battlefield of Fallen Timber, and half way between these two, on the east bank of the river, the site of Fort Meigs.

The most historical sites in the Maumee Valley are the three battlefields that I have enumerated: Fallen Timber, Fort Meigs, and Fort Miami.

Fort Miami was established in 1680 by an expedition sent there by Frontenac, the French Governor of Canada. It was at that time both a military and a trading post, but was abandoned in a few years. In 1785, two years after the treaty of 1783, it was re-occupied by Glencoe, the British Governor of Canada, who held it as a military post. And it was so held by the English at the time when Anthony Wayne defeated the Indian Allies under Little Turtle and Turkey Foot in the battle of Fallen Timber, on August 20, 1794. It was temporarily abandoned by the English in 1795, but again occupied by them later and held until they were finally driven out after the defeat of Proctor and Tecumseh by Harrison, in 1813. The northwestern angle of this Fort and a portion of each adjacent curtain together with the greater part of the demilune in advance of the northern front are still in a fair state of preservation and can be easily traced. The northwestern bastion can be fairly inferred, but the south, or river front, has been destroyed. The site is contained in the town of Miami and covers 5¾ acres.

It was at Fallen Timber on August 20, 1794, that General Anthony Wayne engaged the allied Indian forces under Little Turtle, attacking them with such impetuosity that resistance was impossible. They had chosen their battlefield among the fallen trees, prostrated by a recent hurricane, forming a fortification such as, to the savages, seemed impregnable, and making indeed an almost impassable obstruction to Wayne's mounted troops. But like the wind that had laid low the forest, Wayne came upon the savages, and his soldiers partaking of his own fiery, irresistible courage and impetuosity, swept everything before them. Short as was the battle it was destruction to the savages and decisive of all further Indian warfare in the northwest.

WILLIAM HENRY HARRISON

The battlefield lies on the west bank of the river, and is cultivated for farming purposes. The area comprised within this field is about 2½ acres.

Fort Meigs lies about half way between the two points mentioned, but on the eastern bank of the river. Here it was that General Harrison in the autumn of 1812 set his army to work throwing up the battlements and fortifications which eighty-four years after their construction are, in many respects, as perfect and complete as when they withstood the sieges of Proctor and Tecumseh. The lines of the fortification are all, or nearly all, complete, except where they have been destroyed by roads or cultivation. Unfortunately these comprise some of the most interesting portions, such as the battery at the eastern end of the fort, and the works, of whatever character, at the southwest corner, together with the connection between the latter and the nearest lines are still traceable. The Fort itself covers over fifty-five acres, and in its present state of preservation, is one of the most interesting historical sites in the country, and especially so because here lie buried between twelve hundred and fifteen hundred heroes who fell in and around Fort Meigs and Fort Miami in defense of their flag.

The slaughtered dead of General Harmer's little army lie buried in the low bank of the river at the Ford of the Maumee, now Fort Wayne, where they were cut down by the tomahawk in such numbers that the river was dammed by their bodies, and some of the Indians crossed over upon them without wetting their moccasins.

Wayne's dead lie buried on the most elevated portion of the battlefield of Fallen Timber, over a portion of which passes the public highway, where hourly the traffic of the farmer and of a great city passes without a thought of the sacred dust so ignominiously disturbed.

When General O. M. Poe, of the United States Engineers visited this spot a few years ago, he found the corn-field of a Frenchman covering nearly all the ground where these slaughtered soldiers of nearly a century lie buried. A few of the graves just outside of the corn-rows were still plainly to be seen.

Who were the soldiers who comprised the rank and file of General Anthony Wayne's army? They were the veterans of the American Revolution. The armies of St. Clair, of Harmer, and of Wayne were almost entirely composed of men who had followed Washington and other heroes in the war of the Revolution. It is for that reason that the patriotic societies of the war of the Revolution are urging action for the preservation of these battlefields.

The dead of Fort Meigs lie at four different places, some of them widely separated from the others. There are over one thousand buried in and just outside the walls of the Fort. One grave only, that of Lieutenant Walker, is marked. This by a rough bit of river stone about eight inches square, placed there by the hand of some sorrowing comrade. A few others lie scattered around this spot, but none are marked. They can only be found by close and careful investigation. Two hundred and fifty of the Pittsburg Blues lie across the ravine under the remains of an old wheat stack. Colonel Dudley's gallant six hundred lie east on a high knoll on the bluff of the river, and the ground is so filled and leveled by time that one can hardly dream that from five to six hundred soldiers lie beneath the sod.

The brave and intrepid savage chief, Turkey Foot, who was one of the commanders of the allied tribes at the battle of Fallen Timber is buried near a large rock weighing three or four tons, known as Turkey Foot Rock, and thousands of people visit the spot yearly. I am glad that it is there, for it marks the important battle ground of Anthony Wayne. The lower half of Turkey Foot Rock is imbedded in the soil, by the roadside. The visible portion presents a rounded oblong surface, six feet long, three feet wide, and three and a half feet high. On its top is the track of a turkey's foot rudely carved by an Indian's tomahawk. No Indian ever approached it without placing on it a piece of tobacco. In single file they often passed without halting, each one in silence and sorrow placing his tribute there. After the tribes were sent west of the Mississippi, a few came back to look once more on the fair valley. They never omitted this token of love and honor at Turkey Foot Rock. Shall the pale face fall below the Indian in grateful remembrance? A century has passed since Wayne led our soldiers to victory on this same field and not a single stone marks the resting place of those who fought under his command. Yes, the answer is sure to come in a series of noble monuments, in this valley, worthy of the nation and of the race. One should rise on the brow of Presque Isle hill, in the memory of him who swept like a whirlwind over the field of Fallen Timber.

For nearly twenty years more or less effort has been made to save these graves, and the time has now come when it must be done, or the project abandoned forever. All of these burying places are on private property, and yet this property once belonged to the United States. It was sold in 1817 to private individuals, the Government probably unaware at the time that in this transaction it was bargaining away the bodies of its preservers. Some of the bones have already been unearthed. At Fort Meigs not one of them has, so far, been disturbed, but the owner of the property, Michael Hayes, who so nobly sacrificed a large portion of the best of his farm out of respect for the achievements of his sleeping tenants, is rapidly approaching the end of his own life, and then the property will pass into the hands of several heirs. For nearly a century nature alone has guarded these graves wherein rest a nation's heroes.

> "A tremulous sigh, as the gentle night wind
> Through the forest boughs softly is creeping,
> While the stars up above with their glittering eyes
> Keep guard for the brave that are sleeping."

The burial place on Put-in-Bay Island, where sleep their last sleep those heroes who, under the leadership of the intrepid Perry, fell in that conflict of the lake which forever swept the British from our northern shores, is now marked by a circular inclosure, about thirty feet in diameter,

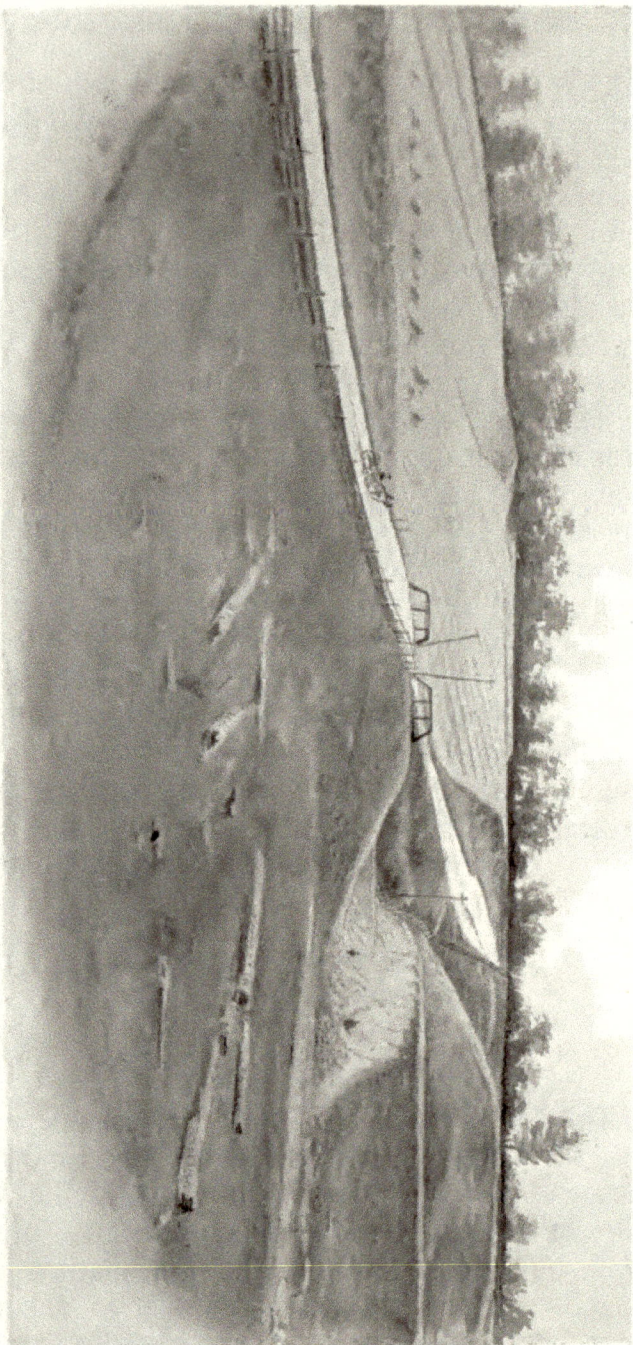
FORT MEIGS, MAUMEE VALLEY, OHIO—1896.

consisting of a few wooden posts in the last stages of decomposition, connected by an iron chain, while a rough stone at the foot of a willow tree is said to mark the exact location of the graves. Sixty feet away is the Bay and between passes a road, sunken some eighteen inches below the level of the ground. It is said that in grading this road some years ago, human bones were excavated and reinterred within the inclosure.

No more important and glorious victory can be found in American history than that of Commodore Perry. As an evidence of this is the magnificent painting hung in the stairway of the Capitol on the Senate side. Yet what shall I say of a Government, which, proud of this matchless achievement, unhesitatingly has spent $25,000 for adornment, and yet, up to the present time, has not contributed one cent to preserve the graves of those who made the adornment possible. A matchless revelation upon canvas, but not one word upon marble.

The grateful citizens of Edinburgh have erected on Colton hill, overlooking the Scottish capital, a memorial of surpassing proportions to commemorate the great victory of Trafalgar. The inscription recites that it is placed there not so much to express their unavailing sorrow for Nelson's death, not to celebrate the matchless glories of his life, but, by his noble example, to teach their sons to emulate what they admire, and, when duty requires, like him, to die for their country. In like spirit, stately shafts should, at no distant day, commemorate these grounds, enriched by the blood of the men who so freely gave their lives at duty's call and which is consecrated by the sleeping dust of our noble brave who to-day rest in nameless graves.

"On fame's eternal camping ground
Their silent tents are spread,
And glory guards, with solemn round,
The bivouac of the dead.

Now wreck, nor change, nor winter's blight,
Now time's remorseless doom
Shall dim one ray of glory's light
That gilds your nameless tomb."

The Influence of the Wayne and Harrison Campaigns on the Settlement of the Northwest.

By the Hon. Stephen A. Northway,

Member of Congress from Ohio.

E VENTS are measured by what is involved in them and what is accomplished, and not by their magnitude. A small affair may mark the foundation of a nation or a nation's liberty, whereas a great event may involve much of magnificence to the world, and yet nothing of consequence to mankind.

There are but few incidents in history that loom above the dead level of events. The battle of Marathon, fought 490 years before Christ, was not a great event, but the Greeks, ten thousand of them, under Miltiades, overcame the Persians and turned back Asiatic invasion. The battle of Chalons, 451 years after Christ, was a small affair, and yet in it Attila, who was called the "Scourge of God," was defeated, and with it ended the Asiatic invasion. The battle of Tours, 732 years after Christ, was a small affair, and yet in it Charles Martel overcame the Saracens and protected forever the glory of Europe. In 1066 William the Norman assumed the English Crown, and from this event sprang the English people and the English tongue. In the battle of Saratoga in 1777, where General Gates defeated General Burgoyne, there were not many soldiers involved, and yet it was the turning point in the American Revolution, for the victory won in that battle brought France as an ally, and so brought victory to our country.

These were small events, yet wonderful in significance to the world.

Away out in the Northwest, beyond the reach of mails, beyond the reach of communication,—in the dark deep forests of Ohio, and Indiana, and Michigan, there was displayed a heroism that will live while immortality shall crown a human being. Men "fought as heroes fought, and died as heroes died," without any of the surroundings of glory that attach to the battle fought in the face of the world. Not a large number of men were involved, but wonderful consequences attached to their acts. The forces involved in the campaigns of Wayne and Harrison were not large, but the mortality stands ready to challenge all history in numbers. The brave men slain in these campaigns outnumber those slain in any other campaign where an equal number were involved. In some of these battles the forces were completely or nearly wiped out; few lived to tell the tale. Brave men leaving their wives and children and homes, marched into a deadly enemy's country, beyond the reach of civilization, and cut their way through dense forests to reach the enemy, and then laid down their lives in defence of their country. These men will yet bloom in immortal fields, and their names will stand like the fixed stars in the firmament, forever to shine upon our nation, while we have a nation.

Wayne's campaign was a short one, extending only from April, 1792, to the treaty of Greenville,

August 3, 1795. During that time he formed his army at Pittsburg, moved across the country to Fort Washington, then across the State of Ohio to the northward, where the battle of Fallen Timber was fought, after having marched hundreds of miles through swamp lands and primitive forests.

All of the Indian tribes of the West or Northwest were banded together in warfare; and when we speak of the Northwest, it must be remembered that the term "Northwest," as used then, did not signify any country west of the Mississippi River.

"Mad" Anthony Wayne carried on a campaign against these Indian tribes. They were banded together for some purpose. Some historians contend that it is a historical fact resting upon very substantial grounds, that England incited the Indian tribes to carry on this warfare. England, when the treaty of 1783 was signed, agreed to evacuate all territory in the Northwest, and to leave this country entirely to ourselves, but failed to do so, for reasons best known to itself. England never ran a very swift race to carry out any such treaty. In the Wayne campaign there were no British soldiers engaged, and yet the battle of Fallen Timber was fought almost under the British guns at Fort Miami, and when the Indian chief retreated, he passed directly under the guns of the British fort, which remained silent. The Indians were put forward to fight that campaign. The British troops very likely believed that the Indians were capable of coping with anything which the Americans could send against them, and if they could but throw a barrier across the Northwest,

all that country westward to the Pacific Ocean
would have been to England what Canada is to-
day.

Wayne's campaigns were fought against the
Indians alone; Harrison's against the Indians and
British combined. Wayne's campaign was a short
but bloody one. The courage of the man who had
fought for his country for seven years in the War
of the Revolution flamed out again in immortal
glory far out in the forests of Ohio.

Wayne negotiated the treaty of Greenville in
1795, and on December 15 of that year, looking
out upon the blue waters, he passed from earth,
and was buried at the foot of the flag at Fort Erie.

I do not know that there is anything very singu-
lar in the nature of the disease that a man should
die of. Yet curiously enough General Wayne died
of the gout; and Little Turtle, thirty years after
he defeated St. Clair, died also of the gout, and
was accorded the burial of a soldier.

The defeat of the Indian tribes broke the spirit
of the tribes. While they were willing and ready
to fight—ready to rush into conflict—they wanted
an ally. Wayne's campaigns had satisfied the
Indians that unaided they could not throw an
effectual barrier in front of the American troops,
and so in the next campaign they fought under
British allies.

And so it was Wayne who first effectually
cleared the way to the great Northwest. See how
instinctively the savages, as well as the British,
anticipated the fact. Their forts were only seven
or eight miles from the city of Toledo. The savages were located directly along the line of the

Ohio River, and here they carried on their depredations; and we are told that from 1783 to 1790
more than fifteen hundred men, women and
children were brutally butchered along the Ohio
River in that region, as they were passing up and
down. Kentucky claims that it holds within its
borders the "dark and bloody ground." Ohio
also claims that title, and while Ohio's braves
fought on Ohio's soil, it gave us the right to say
too that we fought on dark and bloody ground.

I shall not go into the history that leads to the
Harrison campaign. Suffice it to say that we met
with two or three defeats and one surrender.

General Harrison organized his campaign for
what purpose ? The British were holding the line
in the Northwest. At Fort Miami, on the Maumee
River, a little way up from Lake Erie, they were
inciting the savages to warfare. In 1796 the
Northwest Territory contained a population of
about 5,000. Immigrants were seeking homes in
the Northwest. People from Virginia and the
Carolinas came to settle in the Northwest. Ohio
had been admitted to the Union in 1803, the only
State carved out of the Northwest Territory, and
people were naturally looking to that country for
a settlement. Immigration poured in from the
East. It struck Ohio in the northeast corner—that
is, after the settlement of Marietta, in 1788. The
first settlement of the Western Reserve was in
Ashtabula, in the very northeast corner of the
county in the northeast corner of Ohio. Before
there was any settlement at Cleveland, before
there was any county in what is known as the
Western Reserve, in 1796 immigration struck that

county, moving westward.   They moved all along
the shore of the lake.

English ships appeared.   If they could throw a
cordon of men directly across the path of immigration, and check it, the Northwest might yet be
saved.

I need not recount what England did to the
Americans from 1806 to 1813. She denied to us
the right of neutrals, and ours was the only
nation on the globe affected by its orders in
council, taking our men from vessels and impress-
ing them into service everywhere.   We were
weak: England saw its opportunity.   If it could
destroy our commerce and close out from us the
Northwest, it would have an empire; and so it
was necessary that the campaign of Harrison
should be entered upon, and it was entered upon,
and in 1813 the British finally surrendered.   After
the terrible massacre of the River Raisin; after the
battle of Tippecanoe, where Tecumseh was not,
but his twin brother, Prophet, was; after these,
then came the other battles, and the final surrender, and England was obliged to yield its last hold
along the line of the Northwest.

The victory of Wayne destroyed the Indian
power as a power alone.   The victory of Harrison
destroyed the combined Indian and English power
in the Northwest; and while we may have had the
Northwest despite all that, yet those victories as-
suredly gave us the great Northwest in this country,
and made it possible for our nation to place one
hand upon the blue waters of the Atlantic, and the
other upon the rolling waters of the Pacific, and
to say that this is one country and our country,

and that the boast of the American may be as great as that of the Briton who glories that the sun never ceases to shine upon Her Majesty's dominions.

Americans can make the same proud claim for their country, for when the sun goes downward through the gateways of the westward its occidental rays light up the mountains and glaciers of Alaska, while at the same time its oriental rays dance and play along the hill tops and upon the sparkling waters of Maine.

Out of this Northwest saved by the brave Wayne and the gallant Harrison, we have carved five great empires,—Ohio, Indiana, Illinois, Michigan and Wisconsin; and where the Indian war whoop was sounded less than a century ago, to-day there are millions of men and women engaged in peaceful pursuits; surrounded by all the luxuries of civilization; surrounded by all that goes to make life desirable.

Where stood the forests of ninety years ago, we have a great and teeming city; and where the bloody battlefields were ninety years ago, we have beautiful villages and magnificent farms.

What a change! When you stop to think of the result that was wrought by those campaigns, you can ask yourself whence this change, and it is impossible for one to answer it in a single night. Imagination may aid some, but words are powerless. Imagination can picture the continent and the many teeming happy people, but you cannot describe the result. Here we are to-night, Sons of the American Revolution, taking a just pride in the fact that we are descended from the host of

Revolutionary soldiers who made themselves immortal on Revolutionary fields. I can imagine how, years from now, the descendants of yourselves and your children will swell with pride when they think of the fact that along back through the years and away back yonder, some ancestor made himself immortal in defending his country; will take pride in the fact that his children or grandchildren or great-grandchildren banded themselves together as the Sons of the American Revolution or Daughters of the American Revolution, taking pride in the fact that they had a glorious ancestor, and that they were doing what they could to perpetuate his memory.

Let me commend to you your gallant effort, your heroic effort. Preserve the facts of history. Gather them up. Gather up all of them to the end that you may realize the glories of the past, the glories of a common ancestry, the glories of a country made free and grand and great by the heroic efforts of your fathers and your grandfathers, and here pledge anew your devotion to a common country, swearing loyalty to your country that never more shall any hand be lifted against her life unless that hand shall be struck by all the powers of the millions of our countrymen.

The Northwest as Affected by the Treaty of Ghent.

BY THOMAS WILSON, LL.D.,

FORMERLY U. S. CONSUL AT GHENT.

T HE direct cause of the war of 1812 was the exercise by Great Britain of the right of search of American vessels on the high seas.

An indirect cause was Great Britain's interference with the rights of the people on the northwestern frontier in their respective dealings with the Indians. The treaty of 1783 with Great Britain did not bring peace with the Indian tribes on the northwest, and so, while the United States were at peace with Great Britain, the war continued with the Indians, of which the incidents have been described by the other speakers.

In these performances the British soldiery and the British Government stood back of the Indians. It was the policy of the British Government to maintain its frontiers as far south as possible, and then to keep a strip or border of neutral ground between the British and Americans, which should be held by the Indians as a barrier against the Americans. The British thought the Indians could push that frontier farther south on the American territory than England could, and to her, Indian occupation was equivalent to British occupation, for Britain could then use it—not, perhaps, to the exclusion of the Indians, but as outposts and strongholds against the Americans.

The British kept on good terms with the Indians; they made them their allies against the Americans; permitted them to occupy the land, and did not attempt to despoil them of it nor move them to some distant reservation. Therefore they were friends. Great Britain continually acted for her best interests. She sought to use the Indian as a buffer between her people and those of the United States, and her own occupation was thus rendered much safer against attack from the Americans. This was a wisely selfish policy on the part of Great Britain.

In the meanwhile the Indian conflicts with the United States continued or broke out sporadically. The defeats of the Indians each time made them less aggressive, less obstinate, and more easily handled. When the action of Great Britain on the high seas nerved the Government of the United States to take a stand, war was declared.

The United States authorities vainly sought peace, but so long as the British instigated the tribes to war, the savages never thought of ceasing hostilities. The supine indifference of the people at large forced the administration to try every means to obtain peace before adopting the only manly and honorable course, a vigorous war. The frontiersmen looked at the Regular Army with suspicion, and regarded the British and Indians with an equal hatred; they knew that the presence of the British in the Lake Posts meant Indian war, and they knew that whether they behaved well or

ill the Indians would war on them until the tribes
suffered some signal overthrow; meanwhile they
coveted the Indian lands with a desire as simple
as it was brutal. Nor were revenge and the desire
for Indian lands the only motives for aggression;
meaner feelings were mixed with the greed for
untilled prairie and unfelled forests, and fierce long-
ing for blood. It was about this time the idea
was formulated that "the only good Indian was a
dead Indian." Then war was declared and prose-
cuted with such success as we know, until at last
our people got tired of it, and a conference was
agreed upon between the contending nations to
be held at Ghent in the attempt to make a Treaty
of Peace. What was done at that conference,
how the treaty was made, and how it affected the
people of the Northwest, will comprise the rest of
this paper.

The Commissioners on behalf of the United
States were John Quincy Adams, Jonathan Russell,
Albert Gallatin, James A. Bayard and Henry Clay.
They met with the British Commissioners, and
each party presented the points on which they had
been instructed by their respective Governments.

* * * * * * * *

While Mr. Adams was, as the representative of
the New England people, especially those on the
coast, greatly interested in the fisheries, it is not to
be supposed that he neglected or was willing to
give up, the contention against Great Britain in
regard to the Indians. He reports a discussion
with Mr. Goulborn, one of the English Commissioners, from which he became satisfied of the
violence and bitterness of the British against the

Americans, and the determination of its commissioners to adhere to its Indian barrier proposition. Mr. Goulborn declared in unmistakable terms, the belief of himself and his colleagues, that the United States Government, or at least a large number of its people, had designs upon Canada, and their astonishment that Canada had not been attacked at the outset ; that nothing had saved it but the excellent disposition and military arrangements of the governor who commanded there ; that, in order to guard against this in future, it was necessary to make a barrier against our settlement upon which neither party should encroach. He admitted that their proposition of disarmament of the United States upon the lakes had the same purpose—the security of Canada. He declared the Indians to be in themselves a secondary object, but that they could be thus used for the advantage of Great Britain, while as her allies in the war she must make provision to include them in the treaty of peace.

Mr. Adams said, in reply, that wherever the Indians would form settlements and cultivate lands, their possessions were undoubtedly to be respected, and always were respected, by the United States; that some of them had become civilized in a considerable degree, but the greater part of the Indians could never be prevailed upon to adopt this mode of life; their habits, attachments and prejudices were so averse to settlement that they could not reconcile themselves to other conditions than those of wandering hunters. It was impossible for such people ever to be said to have landed possessions. Their only right to land was a right to use it as a hunting ground, and when those lands became necessary or convenient for the purposes of civilized settlement, the system adopted by the United States was, by amicable arrangement with them, to compensate them for renouncing the right of hunting upon them, and for removing to remoter regions better suited to their purposes and mode of life. Between it and taking the lands for nothing, or exterminating the Indians who had used them, there was no alternative. To condemn vast regions of territory to perpetual barrenness and solitude, to the end that a few savages might hunt wild beasts upon it, was a species of game law that a nation descended from the Britons would never endure. It was as incompatible with the moral, as with the physical, nature of things. If Great Britain meant to preclude forever the people of the United States from settling and cultivating these territories, she need not think to do it by means of a treaty. She must formally undertake, and accomplish, the utter extermination of our people. If the Government of the United States should ever submit to such a stipulation, which it was hoped they would not, all its force, and that of Britain combined, would not suffice to carry it into execution. It was opposing a feather to a torrent. The population of the United States in 1810 passed seven million, and now it undoubtedly passed eight. As it continued to increase in such proportions, was it in human experience, or in human power, to check its progress by a bond of paper purporting to exclude posterity from the natural subsistence they would derive from the cultivation of the soil?

Such a treaty, instead of closing the old sources of discussion, would only open new ones. A war thus finished would immediately be followed by another, and Great Britain would ultimately find that she must substitute the project of exterminating the whole American people for that of opposing against them her barrier of savages.

It is useless to repeat the arguments, for and against, made by and before the Commission. They were varied only with the discussion over the British demand for free navigation of the Mississippi and the right of fisheries.

Our Commissioners were pertinacious, full of courage, always polite, kept on good terms with the British Commissioners, discussed minor points when they failed on major, and never allowed the discussions to close on any point with a decision against them, or beyond the possibility of renewal at a more favorable time. They could have broken off the negotiations almost any day, but that was not their policy. In order to succeed they must not only hold the opposing commissioners, but they must convince and convert them—they must overpower them with their arguments or their eloquence, or wheedle or flatter them, or in some way overcome their opposition and secure an agreement.

The treaty as agreed on provided for the establishment of peace, return of possessions, and release of prisoners, but most important for the northwest, it provided for the appointment of commissioners to run the frontier line between the United States and Canada and the British possessions from the Bay of Fundy through the Great Lakes to the Stony Mountains.

The treaty, victory as it was for the United States, is more remarkable for what it omits than what it contains. Every principle which each Government presented at the beginning, was ignored and omitted. No reference was made in the treaty to the right of Great Britain to establish a paper blockade. Nothing was said about the right of search on the high seas, nor the impressment of sailors, nor the extra-territorial rights of British subjects; yet by the arguments of the American commissioners these doctrines were overthrown as effectually as if they had been expressly negatived in the treaty. The British Government has never since claimed them as rights for itself, nor recognized them as rights in others. England's pretensions in this regard were extinguished in the discussion over this treaty as completely as were Spain's by the loss of her great Armada. The contest for equal rights on the high seas, begun by Philip II. 300 years ago in the British channel and continued on the German Ocean amid blood and carnage, was finished in peace at Ghent by the triumph of American diplomacy.

Our Commissioners at Ghent turned their attention to the northern boundary between the two countries, and it was by them forever settled so as to make the foundation of the future greatness of the United States. The Commissioners even builded wiser than they knew; they provided for the acquisition of the Great West which is our pride and strength. What would be our condition or what the value of the Revolution if Great Britain had been successful at Ghent in her contention for an Indian barrier? The Rocky Mountains, Yellowstone Park, the Dakotas, Washington, Idaho, Oregon, with their great agricultural and mineral wealth, would have been lost. Nor is this all; for the United States would have lost the great lakes and a territory which now forms some of our strongest and richest States. The treaty of 1783 gave to Great Britain the free navigation of the Mississippi River from its source to its mouth; the treaty of Ghent by its silence annulled this right.

I have demonstrated the truth of the proposition advanced by your president as a justification for your Society of the Revolution engaging itself in the history of the Northwest, that is, that the war of the Revolution involved and included the war of 1812. I add that the fruits of the Revolutionary victory were secured by the treaty of Ghent, and that these fruits were obtained by the superior management of the United States case by its Commissioners at Ghent. Their positions then taken became crystalized into the acknowledged rights of the American people, admitted by all and denied by none.

www.ingramcontent.com/pod-product-compliance
Lightning Source LLC
Chambersburg PA
CBHW031803090426
42739CB00008B/1142